Understanding Baptism

Mark H. Ballard

Bennington, Vermont

To Cindy and Ben

Understanding Baptism was originally presented in a Sunday Morning Worship Service at Christian Fellowship Baptist Church in Londonderry, NH. The sermon was presented by Pastor Mark H. Ballard just prior to the observance of this holy ordinance. Pastor Ballard later wrote this booklet based upon his previous sermon.

Pastor Ballard stated, "My desire is that the Lord will use this booklet in the lives of thousands of new believers in years to come. I pray that as the reader considers baptism, he will allow himself to be swayed only by God's Holy Word. Furthermore, my prayer is that this booklet will prove to be a useful resource for pastors and church planters in the Northeast."

Dr. Mark H. Ballard serves as the Publisher for Northeastern Baptist Press, and President of Northeastern Baptist College in Bennington, VT. He has served as a faithful pastor, diligent church planter, passionate evangelist, innovative educator, creative and prolific author, pace-setting Baptist leader, and is the husband of Cindy and dad of Benjamin. He graduated Criswell College with his Bachelor's, and Southeastern Baptist Theological Seminary with his M.Div. and Ph.D. Dr. Ballard has filled pulpits, held revival services, and served as a conference speaker in numerous states for more than 40 years.

Should I Be Baptized?

Many new believers find themselves faced with this question on a daily basis. The various church traditions concerning baptism have caused great confusion. Some churches baptize infants; others baptize children and adults while still others will only baptize adults. Some churches sprinkle, some pour, and others insist on immersion. With all the various traditions calling for attention many new believers ask, "Should I be baptized at all?" If one decides to be baptized, they must then question when, where, how and by whom.

The purpose of this brief presentation is not to recount all the various traditions. Nor is it to discuss how the traditions developed throughout history. We will not focus our attention on the traditions nor the practices of any particular church or denomination. Instead, we will focus our attention on the Word of God.

Together, we will seek to gain an understanding of the Biblical expression of baptism. We will begin by considering what the Bible teaches concerning the importance of baptism. Having gained insight into baptism's importance, we will focus our attention on baptism's purpose. Finally, we will turn our attention to the process of baptism.

THE IMPORTANCE OF BAPTISM

Is baptism really necessary? Some would respond to this question with an emphatic, YES! In fact, there are those who claim that without baptism one can have no assurance of Heaven. These folks would tie baptism so close to salvation that no one could possibly be saved from their sin unless they were baptized. However, this position does not pass the Biblical test. It fails on two accounts.

First, the Bible is clear that salvation is not by works – any work – including baptism. (Ephesians 2:8-9; Titus 3:5) Second, we find this position countered from the lips of Jesus Himself. When He was on the cross one of the thieves crucified with Him turned to Him in faith and repentance. The man asked Jesus to remember him in the Lord's Kingdom. Jesus responded, "…today, you will be with me in paradise." (Luke 23:43) There was no time for this man to be baptized. He was about to die a painful death, which he rightly deserved. Yet, when he turned to the Master in repentance and faith Jesus promised him eternal life.

So, is baptism necessary? In light of the facts mentioned above there are many who would respond to that question with a resounding, NO! Clearly, the Bible teaches that one is not required to be baptized in order to be saved from sin. Nor is baptism a prerequisite for Heaven. However, the importance of baptism must not be ignored.

The Bible places a high priority on baptism. This priority can be observed in three distinct ways. First, we see the Biblical importance of baptism in the example of Jesus. Second, we hear the importance of baptism in the command of Jesus. Third, we understand the importance of baptism when we examine the practice of the early church.

The Example of Jesus

> Then Jesus came from Galilee to John at the Jordan to be baptized by him. And John tried to prevent Him, saying, "I need to be baptized by You, and are You coming to me?" But Jesus answered and said to him, "Permit it to be so now, for thus it is fitting for us to fulfill all righteousness." Then he allowed Him. When He had been baptized, Jesus came up immediately from the water; and behold, the heavens were opened to Him, and He saw the Spirit of God descending like a dove and alighting upon Him. And suddenly a voice came from heaven, saying, "This is My beloved Son, in whom I am well pleased." (Matthew 3:13-17)

In Matthew's account we begin to gain a sense of the importance the Bible places on baptism. One day John was down at the river baptizing people in preparation for the coming of the Messiah. Jesus showed up and to John's amazement insisted on being baptized. John knew that Jesus was the perfect Son of God and had no need of baptism. Yet, Jesus insisted saying, "...thus it is fitting for us to fulfill all righteousness." (v. 15)

Through His own baptism Jesus established the importance of the ordinance. He had no sin to repent of, nor any sin to be cleansed. Yet as an act of obedience to the plan of the Father our Lord established the pattern of baptism. He set the example for us to follow. If our Lord thought it important to be baptized how much more should we place a high priority on this beautiful picture of our new relationship with Christ.

The Command of Jesus

A second consideration concerning the importance of baptism can be found in the command of the Lord Jesus. In Matthew 28:18-20 we find a passage of Scripture known as The Great Commission. After Jesus' resurrection He spent some time with His disciples preparing them for the task ahead. He was about to return to His throne in Heaven, but the disciples would be left behind. Notice the words He left with them.

And Jesus came and spoke to them, saying, "All authority has been given to Me in heaven and on earth. Go therefore and make disciples of all the nations, baptizing them in the name of the Father and of the Son and of the Holy Spirit, teaching them to observe all things that I have commanded you; and lo, I am with you always, even to the end of the age." Amen. (Matthew 28:18-20)

Jesus' words include three primary issues the disciples needed to understand. First, He spoke of His power or authority. He wanted them to understand that the Father had given all authority into His hand. He had the right to issue the command they were about to hear.

Second, Jesus spoke to them concerning His plan. This plan was issued to those early followers as a command to be obeyed. This was not optional. Jesus had the authority to issue the command and He expected it to be followed. It was a three-fold imperative. They were to teach all nations, **baptize,** and instruct the new believers in "...all things I (Jesus) have commanded you." From the very beginning the early believers were commanded by Jesus Himself to baptize those who would believe. They were also to ensure that future generations would continue the practice by teaching them to observe all things commanded by the Lord.

Third, Jesus spoke to them concerning His promise. He said, "...and lo, I am with you always, even to the end of the age." Jesus promised that He would be with them as they carried out the task set before them. His presence would ensure wisdom, strength, and ability to carry out His commands.

Jesus is the King of kings and the Lord of lords. He is our Creator, Sustainer, and Redeemer. When He issues a command, it must not be taken lightly. He has commanded that we baptize new believers. Therefore, it is crucial that we follow Him into the waters of baptism without delay.

The Practice of the Early Church

As one studies the book of Acts it becomes abundantly clear that the early believers understood the importance of baptism. Having observed Jesus' example and heard Jesus' command, the church practiced baptism without compromise. The New Testament depicts every new believer as following the Lord in baptism immediately. The only exception to this fact is the thief on the cross, mentioned above.

The practice of immediate baptism of new believers is clearly evident from the earliest days of the church. In Acts chapter two we find 3,000 individuals coming to faith in Christ in one day. The Holy Spirit came upon the disciples of Jesus and they began to share the Gospel with all of Jerusalem. Through the miracle of tongues God enables thousands of people to hear and understand the Gospel message in their native language. Then Peter preached to the multitude. In verse 41 we read:

> Then those who gladly received his word were baptized; and that day about three thousand souls were added to them. (Acts 2:41)

All those who received the gospel message were immediately baptized. Three thousand people trusted their lives to Jesus and then followed Him in obedience by being baptized. From this time forward they were considered to be a part of the church.

Is baptism important? Jesus showed us the importance of baptism by His example. He told us the importance of baptism by His command. The early church demonstrated the importance of baptism by their continual practice. We must conclude that baptism is of utmost importance.

Before you go jump in the water let us consider the purpose of baptism. It is one thing to understand that one should be baptized. It is quite another thing to understand why one should be baptized.

The Purpose of Baptism

A search of the New Testament reveals at least three reasons one should be baptized. One reason you should be baptized is because it is an act of obedience. Another reason is because baptism is an act of identification with Christ. A third reason for baptism is because it is an act of identification with the Church.

Baptism:
An Act of Obedience

Earlier we observed that Jesus commanded his followers to baptize new believers. As we come to the book of Acts it becomes clear that the early believers took Jesus' command very seriously. In chapter 10 we find the Gospel reaching beyond the Jews into the home of Cornelius, a gentile centurion. As Cornelius and his household heard the message of the Gospel, they trusted the Lord and received the Holy Spirit. Upon seeing the work of God in their lives Peter spoke to them.

> And he commanded them to be baptized in the name of the Lord. Then they asked him to stay a few days. (Acts 10:48)

Immediately following their salvation experience, Peter commanded these new believers to be baptized. The command of the Lord passed on to the generation of believers. Following Jesus' ascension every new believer is fully expected to follow the Lord's command to be baptized.

Baptism is a simple act of obedience to the new believer's Lord. If one truly commits their life to Jesus, then they should want to obey Him. Once they understand His command to be baptized, they must respond in obedience.

When I was a young boy growing up, sometimes I struggled with obeying my parents. At times when mother would tell me to take out the trash, feed the dog, clean my room, etc.; I would ask her why. Sometimes she would explain the reason behind her command. However, at times she would simply respond, "Because I am your mother and I told you to do it."

The same could be said of baptism for the new believer. It is great to understand all the issues surrounding baptism, but it ultimately comes down to simple obedience. When asked why one should be baptized sometimes the appropriate response is: "Because Jesus is your Lord and Savior and He said to do it."

Baptism: An Act of Identification with Christ

Although simple obedience is required, understanding the meaning of baptism provides further motivation. The meaning of baptism can be summed up in the word "Identification." Just as your picture on your driver's license identifies you, so the picture of baptism identifies you.

The primary identification that is made in baptism is the identification of the new believer with Jesus Christ. The Apostle Paul discusses this identification in Romans 6.

> Therefore we were buried with Him through baptism into death, that just as Christ was raised from the dead by the glory of the Father, even so we also should walk in newness of life. For if we have been united together in the likeness of His death, certainly we also shall be in the likeness of His resurrection. (Romans 6:4-5)

In this classic passage on baptism Paul clearly establishes the primary purpose of baptism – Identification with Christ. First, we identify with His death. He died, bearing the penalty for our sin. We die to our old way of living. Second, we identify with His resurrection. He rose again, conquering sin, death, and the grave. We are raised to live a new life in Christ.

There is no act that pictures this identification as well as baptism. When one is baptized, he is telling the world that Jesus died and rose again on his behalf. The individual is also telling the world that he has died to self and now lives a new life in Jesus. Thus, the new believer takes a stand and identifies his life with the life of Christ.

Baptism;
An Act of Identification with the Church

When a believer is baptized, he not only identifies himself with Christ but also with Christ's Church. 1 Corinthians 12:12-13 speaks of this secondary identification.

> For as the body is one and has many members, but all the members of that one body, being many, are one body, so also is Christ. For by one Spirit we were all baptized into one body—whether Jews or Greeks, whether slaves or free—and have all been made to drink into one Spirit.

These verses are found in a three-chapter section of I Corinthians dealing with the issues related to spiritual gifts. One of the main themes of chapters 12-14 is that the Church is the Body of Christ. Just as a body is one so the church is one. Just as the body is made up of many parts so the church has many parts (believers). Not all body parts look the same nor do they have the same function. However, as each part works together, the body is able to function properly. The same is true in the local church. We do not all look the same nor act the same but as we work together the church is able to function properly.

In the midst of this discussion, we find verses 12 and 13 relating the Body to baptism. Notice the words of verse 13. The Holy Spirit baptized us all into one body. At the moment you trusted Jesus as your Lord and Savior the Holy Spirit baptized you into the Body of Christ. When you are baptized in the water you are giving an outward picture of the inward reality of what the Lord has done for you. Spirit baptism places you into the Body of Christ; water baptism gives a picture identification of your new role as a member of the local body of believers who baptized you.

Why should you be baptized? You should be baptized because it is an act of simple obedience to your new Lord. You should be baptized because the act identifies you with your Lord. Finally, you should be baptized because the ordinance identifies you with your Lord's church.

THE PROCESS OF BAPTISM

Now that you understand the importance of baptism and the purpose of baptism it is important that you consider the process of the baptism itself. Some churches sprinkle a little water on the head. Some churches pour water on the head. Other churches insist on baptism by immersion. There are multiple reasons for the various methods; however, much of what is done can be traced to the church traditions of various denominations. A discussion of the historical development of the various church traditions is beyond the scope of this work. Instead, we will focus on what the Bible teaches us about the correct process to be followed in baptism.

There are at least three strong indications as to the process of baptism in the New Testament. Once again, we find the starting place to be the example of our Lord. Another indication of the process to be used is found in the example of the early church. A third indicator concerning the correct process for baptism can be found by examining the Greek word from which we received our English word *baptism*.

The Example of Christ

Having already considered Matthew's account of Jesus' baptism let us turn our attention to the parallel account in Mark's Gospel.

> It came to pass in those days that Jesus came from Nazareth of Galilee, and was baptized by John in the Jordan. And immediately, coming up from the water, He saw the heavens parting and the Spirit descending upon Him like a dove. Then a voice came from heaven, "You are My beloved Son, in whom I am well pleased."

There are two key phrases to note in this passage of Scripture that speak to the process of baptism. The first is the phrase, "...in the Jordan." In the accounts of Jesus' baptism, it is significant that we find Jesus and John both in the river. If John sprinkled or poured it would be altogether unnecessary for them to go into the water.

The second phrase which indicates the process of Jesus' baptism is, "...coming up out of the water..." This phrase is a clear indication not only that they were in the water but also that Jesus must have been lowered under the water and that He was raised "up out of the water."

A careful examination of this passage along with its parallel passages indicate that Jesus was clearly baptized by immersion. If He were sprinkled, He would not have needed to go into the Jordan. Nor would He have come up out of the water.

The Example of the Church

Though the example of our Lord should be sufficient for us to understand the process of baptism, let us consider the example of the early church. One of the clearest examples of the process of baptism in the first century church can be found in Acts 8:36-38. In this chapter we find that Philip was sent by the Lord into the wilderness to meet an Ethiopian man. As Philip shared the Gospel of Jesus with the man, he became a believer. Philip then baptized the man. Consider this baptismal experience with me.

> Now as they went down the road, they came to some water. And the eunuch said, "See, *here* is water. What hinders me from being baptized?" Then Philip said, "If you believe with all your heart, you may." And he answered and said, "I believe that Jesus Christ is the Son of God." So he commanded the chariot to stand still. And both Philip and the eunuch went down into the water, and he baptized him.

Notice the phrase "...And both Philip and the eunuch went down into the water," The emphasis of going down into the water is once again clearly observable. Just as with the baptism of our Lord, discussed earlier, it would not have been necessary to go into the water for pouring or sprinkling. However, it is altogether necessary to do so for immersion.

Jesus set the example of baptism by immersion. The early believers not only followed Jesus' example but also passed that example on to us. Clearly, the standard set for baptism is the standard of immersion. Note with me one other indication of the proper process to be followed in believer's baptism.

The Definition of the Word

Every time you find the word baptism in the New Testament it is a translation of the Greek word, *Baptidzo*. In fact, it is actually not a translation but a transliteration. When we translate a word from one language to another, we give its definition. However, when we transliterate a word, we simply take the word from one language and put it into the letters of another language.

For example, my name is Mark. If you were to take my English name and translate it into Spanish you would use the Spanish words that mean, "strong defender", for that is the definition of my name. However, if you were to transliterate my name into Spanish you would call me, *Marcos*, which is the normal practice.

In the English New Testament, the Greek word *baptidzo* has been brought into English through the process of transliteration. You can clearly see the connection between the two words. However, the dictionary meaning of *baptidzo* is "to immerse, to place under completely, to submerge."

If Jesus had desired us to be sprinkled, He would have used the Greek word *rantidzo*. If He had wanted water to be poured on us, He would have used the Greek word *ekkeo*. However, there is not one place in the New Testament where these words are used in relation to the first act of obedience following salvation. Over and over again the Lord chose the Greek word *baptidzo*. The choice of the word clearly indicates that God's plan is that we be immersed or placed completely under the water.

Having gained an understanding of the purpose of baptism earlier this makes complete sense. If the primary meaning of baptism is identification with Christ, His death, and His resurrection, then immersion is preferred. Sprinkling does not identify the new believer with the death and resurrection of Jesus. Pouring does not identify us with the death and resurrection of Jesus. However, immersion clearly pictures the life, death, burial, and resurrection of our Lord. Thus, through immersion we clearly identify ourselves with our Lord and Savior Jesus Christ.

When Should I Be Baptized?

Now that you understand the importance of baptism, the purpose of baptism and the process of baptism you may be asking yourself when you should be baptized. Once again, we find that there are a few different church traditions concerning this question. Some believe that you should be baptized as an infant. Some say that only adults should be baptized. Still others say that the teenage years are the best time for such an event.

Again, we will not turn to church traditions for an answer to this question. Instead, we will consider the

New Testament examples before us. In every instance we have considered we find that baptism always follows a personal choice of faith. In fact, EVERY instance of baptism in the Scriptures follows personal faith. That is why the act is many times called, "believer's baptism."

Thus, when should one be baptized? One should be baptized at the time of their salvation experience. When you come to the place of realizing that you have been separated from God by your sin, that Jesus died to pay the penalty for your sin, that He rose again to win the victory over your sin. When you turn from sin and self by placing your complete trust in the Lord Jesus Christ. At this point in time in your life you should follow the Lord in baptism.

Notice that if one must be a believer to be baptized then infants are automatically precluded. The question then comes, "At what age can a person be baptized?" The answer is different for every individual. Some children gain a clear understanding of their need for salvation at a young age. These children could be baptized as soon as they trust their lives to Jesus. Other children fail to understand their need until the pre-teen or teen years. Whatever the age, once this need is understood and the choice is made to trust one's life to Christ, the new believer can and should follow the Lord in baptism.

You may ask, "What if I was baptized as an infant?" If this were the case for you then I would counsel you to first consider your current understanding. Do you understand your need for salvation in Jesus? Have you turned from sin and self, trusting your life to Jesus as your Lord and Savior? Then you need to follow the Scriptural pattern of believer's baptism as soon as possible.

Why don't you join the Ethiopian eunuch we read about earlier? Go to the pastor and ask him to baptize you in the name of the Father, and the Son and the Holy Spirit. Remember the words of the Ethiopian man. "See here is water, what hinders me from being baptized?" Let me ask. What hinders you from being baptized?